25.20

ENDANGERED MANATEES

Bobbie Kalman & Hadley Dyer

Crabtree Publishing Company

www.crabtreebooks.com

Earth's Endangered Animals Series
A Bobbie Kalman Book

Dedicated by Hadley Dyer
For Amy Dyer, with much affection

Editor-in-Chief
Bobbie Kalman

Writing team
Bobbie Kalman
Hadley Dyer

Substantive editor
Kathryn Smithyman

Project editor
Molly Aloian

Editors
Robin Johnson
Kelley MacAulay
Rebecca Sjonger

Design
Katherine Kantor
Samantha Crabtree (front cover)

Production coordinator
Heather Fitzpatrick

Photo research
Crystal Foxton

Consultant
Patricia Loesche, Ph.D., Animal Behavior Program,
Department of Psychology, University of Washington

Illustrations
Barbara Bedell: page 6 (top)
Katherine Kantor: pages 5, 6 (bottom), 12-13
Bonna Rouse: back cover, pages 11, 16
Margaret Amy Salter: page 30

Photographs
© Whitehead, Fred / Animals Animals - Earth Scenes: page 28
© Lake County Museum/CORBIS: page 20
Index Stock: Frank Staub: pages 4-5; Shirley Vanderbilt: page 10
Minden Pictures: Fred Bavendam: pages 12-13, 19
Naturepl.com: Brandon Cole: page 3; Jurgen Freund: page 18;
    Doug Perrine: pages 14-15; Todd Pusser: page 17
Michael Patrick O'Neill/Photo Researchers, Inc.: page 27
SeaPics.com: Marc Chamberlain: page 29; Doug Perrine: front cover,
    pages 7, 8, 23, 24, 25; Masa Ushioda: page 9
U.S. Geological Survey, Sirenia Project, R.K. Bonde: page 21
Other images by Corel, Digital Stock, and Digital Vision

Crabtree Publishing Company

www.crabtreebooks.com   1-800-387-7650

Cataloging-in-Publication Data
Kalman, Bobbie.
  Endangered manatees / Bobbie Kalman & Hadley Dyer.
     p. cm. -- (Earth's endangered animals)
  Includes index.
  ISBN-13: 978-0-7787-1868-0 (rlb)
  ISBN-10: 0-7787-1868-9 (rlb)
  ISBN-13: 978-0-7787-1914-4 (pbk)
  ISBN-10: 0-7787-1914-6 (pbk)
  1. Manatees--Juvenile literature. 2. Endangered animals--Juvenile literature.
I. Dyer, Hadley. II. Title.
  QL737.S63K35 2006
  599.55'168--dc22

                                                    2005036718
                                                          LC

**Published in
the United States**
PMB16A
350 Fifth Ave.
Suite 3308
New York, NY
10118

**Published
in Canada**
616 Welland Ave.
St. Catharines, Ontario
Canada
L2M 5V6

**Published in the
United Kingdom**
White Cross Mills
High Town, Lancaster
LA1 4XS
United Kingdom

**Published
in Australia**
386 Mt. Alexander Rd.
Ascot Vale (Melbourne)
VIC 3032

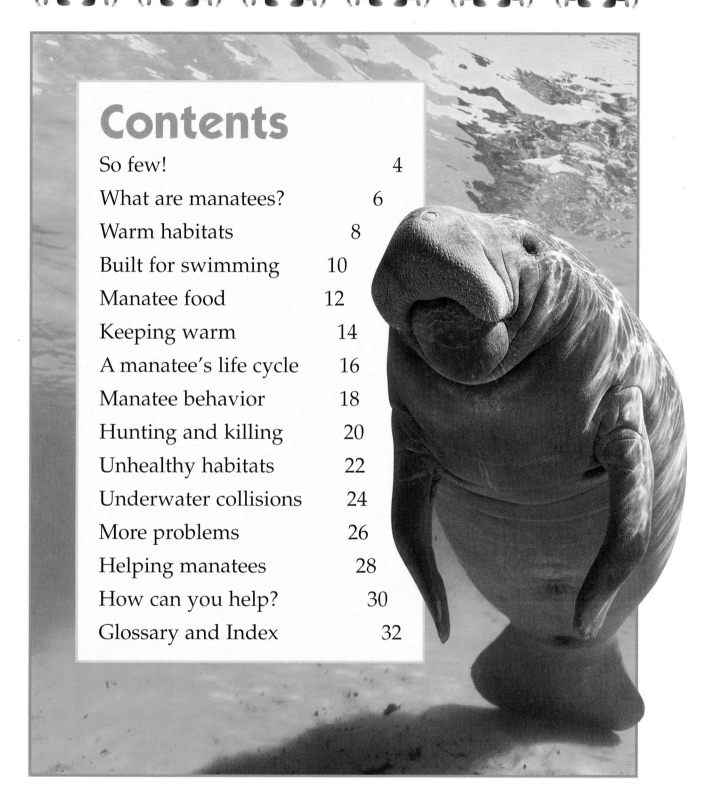

Contents

So few!

Manatees have been living on Earth for millions of years. Once, there were many manatees, but today manatees are in danger. Some scientists believe manatees are **vulnerable**, whereas others believe manatees are **endangered**.

Manatees need help!

All scientists agree that manatees face many dangers in the **wild**, or natural areas that are not controlled by people. If people do not work together to protect manatees in the wild, these animals may one day become **extinct**.

4

Words to know

Scientists use certain words to describe animals in danger. Some of these words are listed below.

vulnerable Describes animals that may soon become endangered

endangered Describes animals that are in danger of dying out in the wild

critically endangered Describes animals that are at high risk of dying out in the wild

extinct Describes animals that are no longer living anywhere on Earth or animals that have not been seen in the wild for at least 50 years

What are manatees?

Manatees are **mammals**. Mammals are **warm-blooded** animals. The body temperatures of warm-blooded animals stay about the same no matter how hot or cold their surroundings are. Mammals have **backbones**, and most are covered with fur or hair. A backbone is a row of bones in the middle of an animal's back. Baby mammals **nurse**, or drink milk from the bodies of their mothers.

Marine mammals

Manatees are **marine mammals**. Marine mammals are mammals that live and find food mainly in oceans. Whales and seals are other marine mammals.

The sirenians

Manatees belong to an **order**, or group, of animals called **sirenians**. There are two kinds of sirenians— manatees and dugongs. All dugongs are vulnerable. Until about 250 years ago, there was a third kind of sirenian called the Steller's sea cow, but this animal is now extinct.

Dugongs live in oceans around Australia.

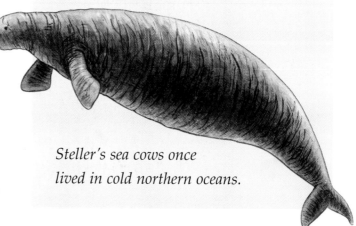

Steller's sea cows once lived in cold northern oceans.

Three species

There are three **species**, or types, of manatees—Amazonian manatees, West African manatees, and West Indian manatees. Amazonian manatees live in South America, in the Amazon River and its **channels**. West African manatees live along the west coast of Africa, from Senegal to Angola. West Indian manatees live in waters around North and South America.

Subspecies

There are two **subspecies**, or kinds, of West Indian manatees— Antillean manatees and Florida manatees. Antillean manatees live mainly in the waters in the **Caribbean**. Florida manatees live mainly in the waters around the state of Florida in the United States.

Most Amazonian manatees have white or pink patches on their chests.

Warm habitats

Florida manatees often live in oceans around Florida, where many people live. As a result, many people—including scientists—know more about Florida manatees than they know about other manatee species.

Manatees live in parts of the world that have warm **climates**. The temperatures of the waters in which they live are warm year round. All species of manatees live in similar **habitats**. A habitat is the natural place where an animal lives. Manatees live in warm, shallow bodies of water, such as slow-moving rivers, **canals**, bays, lagoons, and **coastal waters**. Coastal waters are the parts of oceans that are near land.

Home alone

Manatees spend most of their lives alone. Each manatee lives in its own **home range**. A home range is the area within an animal's habitat in which it lives, finds food, and has babies. Manatees sometimes gather together in areas where there is a lot of food. They also huddle together in warm spots in the ocean when the weather turns cool.

West African manatees live in coastal waters, in rivers, and in streams.

Salty or fresh?

Oceans contain **salt water**, whereas lakes and rivers contain **fresh water**. Amazonian manatees live only in fresh water. West Indian manatees and West African manatees live in both salt water and fresh water.

When they are searching for food, West Indian manatees and West African manatees swim from salty ocean habitats to freshwater habitats, such as rivers, lakes, and **estuaries**. An estuary is a body of water that forms where a river meets an ocean.

Built for swimming

Manatees have bodies that are built for life in water. Their bodies are **fusiform**, or sleekly shaped. Having fusiform bodies helps manatees move quickly through water. Manatees use their paddle-like **flukes**, or tails, to push themselves forward. Layers of **blubber**, or fat, on their bodies help keep manatees warm. Manatees have thick, gray skin. Unlike mammals that live on land, manatees have little hair on their bodies.

*Manatees live under water, but they must swim to the surface to breathe air. When manatees dive, their **nostrils** close to keep out water. Nostrils are openings on the nose.*

A manatee's body

Whiskers are hairs on a manatee's snout that help the animal feel its surroundings.

nostril

*A manatee has small eyes. Each eye is protected by a **membrane**, or a thin layer of skin.*

Large lungs

Manatees have large **lungs** in their chests. Lungs are body parts that take in and let out air. Each lung holds a lot of air. Large lungs allow manatees to stay under water for long periods of time.

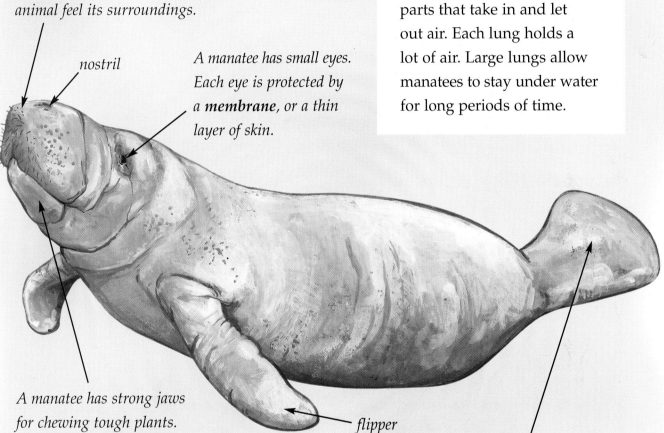

A manatee has strong jaws for chewing tough plants.

flipper

Handy flippers

Manatees have two front **flippers**. They use their flippers to steer their bodies as they swim through water. They also use their flippers to push food into their mouths.

A manatee's fluke is very powerful. A manatee swims by moving its fluke up and down.

11

Manatee food

Manatees eat mainly sea grasses and **algae**. Sea grasses grow on the bottom of warm, shallow waters. Some also float on or near the surface of the water. Algae are plantlike living things that also grow in sunlit, shallow waters. Manatees also eat plants that grow along shores. They sometimes swallow fish or other animals, such as snails or small crabs, that are attached to the plants they eat.

Lips that grasp

Manatees have powerful jaw muscles and large lips. Their lips are **prehensile**. Prehensile body parts are able to grasp. Manatees use their strong jaws and lips to grasp and pull sea grasses from the ocean floor.

A fully grown adult manatee eats 100 to 150 pounds (45-68 kg) of food each day.

12

Mighty molars

Manatees eat for six to eight hours each day! They do not have front teeth for biting. Instead, they have rows of **molars**, or back teeth, for chewing and grinding food. Over time, the molars wear down. When a manatee's molar wears down, it falls out and leaves a gap. A molar from the back of the manatee's mouth moves forward to fill the gap. New molars grow at the back of the jaw so that there are always teeth to replace those that have fallen out.

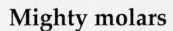

13

Keeping warm

Manatees are slow-moving animals that produce little heat in their bodies. Their blubber helps keep them warm, but it is not thick enough to keep them warm in cold water. Even in tropical regions, the temperatures can drop, and the water can become cool. When the water in which manatees live becomes cool, manatees gather together in warm spots.

Migrating manatees

Some manatees have home ranges in areas where the seasons change. In winter, the waters in their home ranges becomes cool for several weeks each year. As soon as the temperature drops, these manatees **migrate** to warmer waters. Some species travel up to 500 miles (805 km) from their home ranges to reach warmer waters!

These manatees have gathered together in a warm spot in the water. They will wait for the weather to become warm before they leave to find food.

A manatee's life cycle

Every living thing goes through a set of **stages**, or changes, called a **life cycle**. A manatee's life cycle begins when it is born. A mother manatee usually gives birth only to one **calf**, or baby, at a time. As it grows, the calf becomes a **juvenile**, or young, manatee. The animal continues to grow until it is **mature**, or an adult. When a manatee is mature, it can **mate**, or join together with another manatee to make babies.

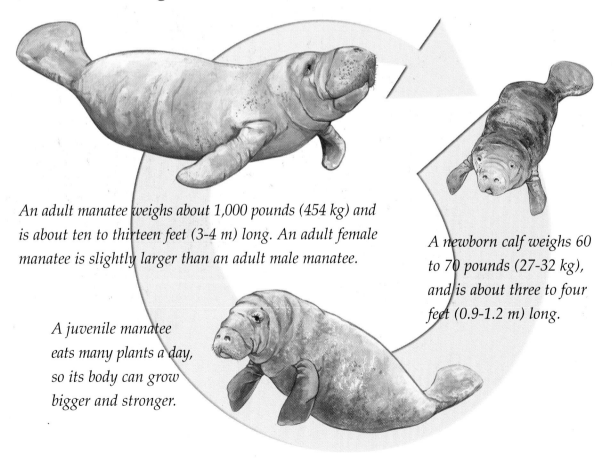

An adult manatee weighs about 1,000 pounds (454 kg) and is about ten to thirteen feet (3-4 m) long. An adult female manatee is slightly larger than an adult male manatee.

A newborn calf weighs 60 to 70 pounds (27-32 kg), and is about three to four feet (0.9-1.2 m) long.

A juvenile manatee eats many plants a day, so its body can grow bigger and stronger.

Growing up

A few hours after a manatee calf is born, it can swim on its own. It nurses often. When the calf is between one and three months old, it starts eating plant foods, but it continues to nurse until it is up to three years old. Calves stay close to their mothers for about three years. Juvenile manatees over two years old spend time on their own, however. Eventually, they find home ranges of their own. Female manatees become mature at age four or five, whereas males become mature at about age nine.

This West Indian manatee calf is drinking milk from its mother's body.

Manatee behavior

Manatees **communicate**, or send messages, in different ways. They may **vocalize**, or make noises. The noises sound like squeaks, squeals, and chirps. Manatees vocalize to express anger or fear, to warn other manatees of danger, to attract partners, or to call other manatees. Manatees also communicate by touching one another with their bodies. They may show affection by nuzzling, chasing, and bumping.

A trail of scent

A female manatee tells males that she is ready to mate by rubbing her **scent**, or smell, onto objects in the water, such as rocks. Several males may follow the scent trail to the female. They form a group called a **mating herd**. A mating herd includes one female and as many as 22 males. The group stays together for up to one month.

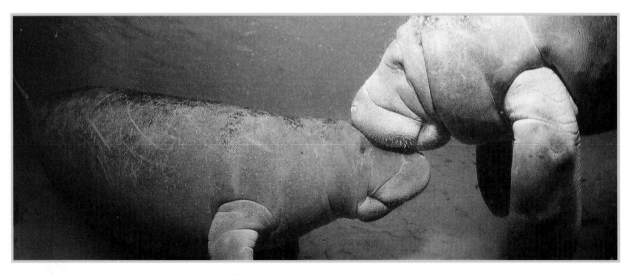

Mothers and their calves vocalize often to keep track of one another.

Time for sleep

When manatees are awake, they usually swim to the water's surface every few minutes to breathe. Manatees sleep often. While sleeping, manatees drift to the bottom of the water on their backs or on their stomachs. They rise to the surface every ten minutes or so to breathe. Scientists are not sure if manatees wake up when they come to the surface to breathe.

This sleeping West Indian manatee will have to breathe very soon!

Hunting and killing

During the 1700s and 1800s, hunters from many countries were killing sea otters and fur seals. The hunters soon discovered that slow-moving manatees and other sirenians were easy to hunt. The hunters killed huge numbers of sea cows, manatees, and dugongs and ate their meat. In fact, they hunted Steller's sea cows to extinction by 1768. Having fresh meat allowed the hunters to stay out on their boats and hunt for long periods of time. These hunters drastically reduced the **populations** of all species of manatees.

Continued killing

Commercial hunters hunt animals in order to sell them. Commercial hunters continue to hunt manatees and sell them for their meat. Many people also kill manatees for sport. Since manatee populations are so low, many people believe that no more manatees should be killed.

Caught in nets

Manatees sometimes get caught accidentally in fishing gear, such as nets. Some fishers kill the manatees to keep them from tearing fishing nets. Other fishers try to release the manatees from the nets. Many manatees still become injured from the nets, however.

This West Indian manatee has been caught in a net and must be returned to the water immediately in order to survive.

Unhealthy habitats

Today, the greatest threat to manatees is people **polluting** their habitats. Polluted habitats contain harmful or poisonous substances. People pollute water by dumping garbage, chemicals, and other wastes into it. The chemicals are in **detergents, fertilizers** and other products that people use in and around their homes and farms. Factories also dump chemicals into manatee habitats. Manatees that live in polluted habitats can become sick or even die.

Seagrass beds

Some kinds of sea grasses spread over large areas. Large areas of seagrasses are called **seagrass beds**. In many areas, polluted water flows into oceans near seagrass beds and kills them. Seagrass beds are also damaged when oil or gasoline spills or leaks out of boats.

Spreading silt

When seagrass beds die, the areas become bare and the **silt** becomes loose. Silt is very fine dirt and sand. The loose silt spreads to nearby areas. If it **settles**, or lands, on another seagrass bed, it smothers and kills that seagrass bed, as well.

*Seagrass contains **nutrients** that manatees need to stay alive.*

Underwater collisions

Many people spend time boating through the waters in which Florida manatees live. As a result, many Florida manatees are hit by boats.

Manatees have few natural **predators**. Predators are animals that hunt other animals for food. The actions of people put manatees in great danger. Millions of people live in or visit areas near manatee habitats. Many of the people act in ways that harm manatees.

Too low

Manatees have good hearing, but they cannot hear the low sounds that certain boat **motors** make in water. As a result, manatees are often hit by boats because they cannot move away from the boats in time. When manatees are hit by careless boat drivers, they are injured or killed by the boat **propellers** and motors.

Stop the scars

Many Florida manatees, such as the one shown above, have scars on their bodies from being hit by boats. To help prevent manatees from being hit, speed limits have been set in some of their habitats.

Boaters must travel slowly on these waters. By traveling slowly, drivers have time to see manatees and steer around them. Other **regulations**, or rules, limit the number of boats that are allowed in an area at the same time.

More problems for manatees

In Florida, many people enjoy visiting manatees when the animals gather together in winter. In fact, some people swim with the manatees. Too much contact with people can harm manatees, however. Some people poke, ride, or tie ropes to the manatees. The behavior of these people often causes manatees to avoid the warm waters they need in winter. The manatees then become too cold and die. Mothers and calves that swim with people may become separated from one another. Without their mothers, the babies also die.

Unfortunately, people swim with manatees, even though it is not always safe for the manatees.

What if they close?

People sometimes help certain wild species, even when they do not intend to do so. In Florida, several electric power plants have been built near bodies of water, such as canals. The power plants use water to cool their steam pipes. After being used and pumped out again, the canal water is warm, and manatees love to swim in it! Manatees often move to artificially warmed areas for the winter months. Some people worry about what would happen to manatees that live near power plants if the plants were to close down, however.

Blocked paths

Manatees that swim in rivers and canals are sometimes trapped or crushed by **canal locks**. A canal lock is a huge gate that controls the flow of water in a waterway. **Dams** may also cause problems for manatees. A dam is a barrier that holds back water and raises its level. The water is often used to produce electricity. If people build dams and canal locks along manatee **migration routes**, the animals will be unable to reach warmer waters.

27

Helping manatees

Scientists around the world study manatees and their behavior. By studying manatees, scientists learn how to protect them.

Many people are concerned about manatees and are working hard to keep them safe. **Conservation organizations** are groups of people who save animals and their habitats. Some conservation organizations rescue injured manatees. When the manatees are healed, they are released back into the wild. The organizations also educate people about how to protect manatees.

Protected areas

Conservation organizations have also created manatee **sanctuaries**. The sanctuaries are areas of manatee habitats that are off-limits to people. Sanctuaries employ **rangers**. Rangers are people who patrol protected areas to keep manatees and other animals safe from hunters. Manatees in sanctuaries can rest, feed, and have babies without being disturbed.

Some protection

Today, it is **illegal**, or against the law, to hunt, capture, or disturb manatees in most of the countries where they live. Unfortunately, illegal hunting continues in parts of West Africa, the Caribbean, and South America. Some countries do not have enough police or rangers to protect the manatees that live there. Many areas, such as the Amazon River, are difficult to patrol because they are hard for people to reach.

In the state of Florida, it is illegal to disturb manatees.

29

How can you help?

The best way for you to help manatees is to continue learning about them and about other endangered animals. You can then teach others interesting facts about these animals. A great way to teach other people is by creating artwork. You can draw pictures that show different manatee movements, for example. Manatees may move slowly, but they can roll over, do somersaults, and swim upside down. Display your manatee artwork on a large piece of cardboard for other students in your school to see. Then ask them to draw pictures.

More on manatees

You can find information about manatees in this book, in other books, in magazines, and on the Internet. Try the following websites:

• Take a manatee quiz on the Save the Manatee Club site: **www.savethemanatee.org/quiz.htm**

• Send a manatee postcard at National Geographic for Kids. First click on "creature features" then click on "Manatees, West Indian" **www.nationalgeographic.com/kids**

Glossary

Note: Boldfaced words that are defined in the text may not appear in the glossary.

canal A waterway built by people, which allows boats to travel inland

Caribbean A region that includes the Caribbean Sea, its islands, and the surrounding coasts

channel A body of water that joins together two larger bodies of water

climate The long-term weather conditions in an area, including temperature, rainfall, and wind

detergent A chemical that is used to wash things

fertilizer Chemicals that people use to help plants grow

fresh water Water that does not contain salt

fusiform Describing something that is wider in the middle than it is at both ends

migrate To move from one area to another for a certain period of time

migration route The path between a migrating animal's home range and the place where it moves in cold weather

motor A machine that powers a vehicle

nutrients Natural substances that help animals grow and develop

population The total number of one species of animal living in a particular area of the world

propeller A machine that pushes a boat through water, and which is made up of a spinning part and two or more blades

salt water Water that contains salt

Index

1 2 3 4 5 6 7 8 9 0   Printed in the U.S.A.   5 4 3 2 1 0 9 8 7 6